SCHOLASTIC

50 Fill-In Math Word Problems

ALGEBRA

Grades 4–6

by Bob Krech and Joan Novelli

New York • Toronto • London • Auckland • Sydney
Mexico City • New Delhi • Hong Kong • Buenos Aires

Teaching *Resources*

Thanks to Andrew and Faith for laughing

Editor: Joan Novelli
Cover design by Jason Robinson
Interior design by Holly Grundon
Interior illustrations by Mike Moran

ISBN-13: 978-0-545-07487-2
ISBN-10: 0-545-07487-8

Contents

Fill-In Math Word Problems

About This Book

When we learn to read, we learn to recognize the letters of the alphabet, we practice letter-sound relationships, and we learn punctuation, but what it's all about is eventually being able to read text. A similar situation exists in math. We learn how to recognize and write numerals, what the symbols mean, numerical order, and operations like multiplication and division, but what it's all about is what you can do with these skills—applying what you know to solve problems. *50 Fill-In Math Word Problems: Algebra* provides lots of funny stories to fill in—and some very interesting problems to solve.

What Are Fill-In Math Word Problems?

A fill-in math word problem is a funny story with a math problem waiting to happen. Most of the word problem is already supplied except for a few key words and numbers that have been removed and replaced with blanks. It's up to the students to fill in those blanks with missing nouns, verbs, adjectives, and other types of words—just like in some other popular word games. The difference is that this game is missing some numbers as well. When your students supply the missing numbers along with the words, they suddenly have a wacky, math word problem that's fun to read and solve!

Why Use Fill-In Math Word Problems?

Traditional math word problems can provide a meaningful context for students to apply their skills, but sometimes the problems can be a bit boring. Remember trying to figure out when the two trains would pass each other? That won't happen with *50 Fill-In Math Word Problems*. Students help create these wacky word problems, which provide for plenty of good problem-solving practice with grade-appropriate math skills and concepts. Have fun while doing math? Absolutely!

Teaching With Fill-In Math Word Problems

The stories in this book are organized by skills, beginning with those that provide practice with repeating patterns. You can choose a fill-in story to use with the entire class, or select as many as needed to match different ability levels of students. For instance, you might have some students who would benefit from practice with repeating patterns, while others may be ready for problems that require working with variables. (For connections to the math standards, see Meeting the Math Standards, page 12.) Whatever the need, there is a set of fill-in stories to support it. Following is the order of stories by skill area.

- Repeating Patterns
- Growing Patterns
- Drawing or Graphing Patterns
- Using Variables
- Expressions and Formulas
- Equations and Properties

Teaching Tips

When teaching with the stories in this book, be sure to review and reinforce the following strategies with students.

- Identifying patterns helps us make predictions about what comes next. When working on problems that involve patterns and algebra, lists and tables are useful for organizing information.

- Organize numbers in rows, columns, or streams that are near one another so that you can easily detect relationships among the numbers. For example, let's say you make three two-point baskets in your first basketball game of the season, and double that number in the next game. In each of the next three games, you double the number of baskets from the previous game. How many points will you have scored after five games? To figure out the answer, you could organize the data in columns (see right).

Game	Baskets	Points
1	3	6
2	6	12
3	12	24
4	24	48
5	48	96

- If someone asks how many points you might score in game 6, we could answer 192 because we've seen the relationship between the number of baskets and the number of points. This is a growing pattern, where the numbers increase.

- A table or chart is also helpful for arranging and keeping track of information about patterns that repeat, such as the teacher who wears blue sneakers on odd days and red sneakers on even days. To find out what color sneakers this teacher will be wearing on Thursday, if Monday is March 10, you might make a chart (see right).

Date	Color
Mon. 3/10	red
Tues. 3/11	blue
Wed. 3/12	red
Thurs. 3/13	blue

(Answer = blue, because Thursday would be March 13, which is an odd-numbered day.)

Modeling the Process

Before expecting students to complete stories on their own, model the process of filling in the blanks for a story and solving the problem. Use an overhead to project the story so students can follow along. Invite a student to help you out, and follow these steps:

1. Starting at the beginning of the story, read the prompts for the fill-ins—for example, "plural noun." Write in the noun your helper suggests—for example, *basketballs*.

2. When you have filled in all of the blanks, read aloud the story, beginning with the title.

3. Read aloud the problem in "Solve This!" and think aloud as you use information from the story to solve the problem. (This is a good time to model how to use the Fantastic Five-Step Process. See page 9 for more information.)

How to Fill in the Blanks

Each fill-in math word problem requires students to fill in a set of words and numbers to complete the story. They will then use some of the information they provide to solve the problem. Following is more detailed information about how to fill in the blanks.

Choosing Words

From singular and plural nouns to verbs and adjectives, different kinds of words are required to fill in the blanks of the stories. Review each type of word with students, using the Word Choice Chart (page 13) as a guide. To help students create their own handy references, have them complete the third column of their chart with additional examples of each type of fill-in. They can refer to this when completing stories as a reminder of what kinds of words they can use. You might also consider transferring the descriptions and examples to a wall chart for easy reference.

Note that, at times, students will also have to fill in some other types of words, such as the name of a girl, boy, or famous person, a type of animal, or a color. These are not included in the chart as they are already specific enough to support students in their word choice. When you introduce any new story to students, just take a moment to review all of the types of words they may need to use.

Choosing Numbers

Some stories specify a range for numbers—for example, "The Big Test" (page 20) invites students to choose a number from 1 to 100. Others, such as "Concert Tour" (page 25), ask for more specific numbers, in this case "triple-digit number ending with 4." You may choose to let students fill in numbers according to the directions in the stories as is, or you can modify the parameters to provide for differentiation of instruction, individualizing the problems for students by using the number ranges that make sense for them. If you do change the fill-in prompts in this way, be sure to check for other numbers in the story that may also need to be changed. However, keep in mind that leaving the number size open-ended to some extent is an interesting option and will provide information as to students' ability to work with different-size numbers.

Lesson Formats

There are many ways to use the stories in *50 Fill-In Math Word Problems* in your classroom. Suggested lesson formats follow.

1. Problem-Solving Partners

Have students pair up. Make copies of a fill-in story and distribute to one student in each pair. These students are the Readers. Without revealing the title (or any parts) of the story, Readers ask their partners for the missing words and numbers in order ("present-tense verb," "color," "single-digit number greater than 1," and so on) and fill in the appropriate blanks with their partner's responses. When all the blanks are filled in, the Reader reads the completed story. The resulting silly story now contains a math word problem! Partners solve the problem (together or independently), sharing strategies and checking their answers.

2. Class Stories

Choose a story and let students take turns supplying words and numbers to fill in the blanks (again, just read the fill-in prompts in turn, but do not reveal the story at this point). When the story is complete, read it to the class. Have students take notes on the numbers in the story and the problem they need to solve. (Or write this information on chart paper for them.) Students can work together as a class, with a partner, or independently to solve the problem. As a follow-up, let students share answers and discuss problem-solving strategies.

3. Story Switcheroo

After students fill in the blanks for a story with a partner, make copies and distribute to the class for extra practice or homework. Twenty different versions of one story mean 20 different problems to solve! And students will love seeing their work used as a teaching tool!

4. Math Practice Pages

Invite pairs of students to create stories for a binder full of practice pages. They fill in the stories as described in "Problem-Solving Partners" (see above), but solve the problem and write an explanation on the back of the paper. For extra practice, students can take a story from the binder, solve the problem (on a separate sheet of paper), and check their answer on the back. They can then return the story to the binder.

5. Create New Stories

Creating new fill-in stories is another option for practicing math skills—and a motivating way to connect writing and math. Using the stories in this book as models, invite students to write their own wacky, fill-in math stories. With students' permission, copy the stories and distribute to the class for homework (or in-class practice). On the following page you'll find tips to share with students as they plan and write their stories.

Tips for creating fill-in math stories:

- Identify a skill area and write this at the top of the paper. You may choose to specify a skill area for students, such as "Growing Patterns," or leave this up to students to decide.

- Brainstorm story ideas. Everyday events, such as playing kickball or going shopping, can make for very funny stories. Think about how algebra might fit into the story. For example, anytime something is purchased in a quantity, there is probably going to be a relationship or pattern. If there's a special at the pet store on your cat's favorite food, with a savings of $0.75 per can, it might pay to stock up. You can begin to think algebraically when you consider that N x $0.75 = amount you will save, when N represents the number of cans of cat food you purchase.

- Write a draft of your story. Do not try to make your story "funny." Just write about the event as if you were telling someone else about it. When you're finished, underline some of the verbs, adjectives, and nouns, then erase the original word. Label the type of word or number beneath each blank. Be sure to set up a math problem in the story.

- Write the problem to be solved in the space labeled "Solve This!" Solve the problem yourself to make sure it works.

- Draw a picture to illustrate the story.

Review of Terminology

Before using the stories in this book, review the following terms, and make sure students understand them as they relate to completing the stories and solving the math problems.

Core of a Pattern: The core is the part that repeats again and again—for example, in the pattern green, green, yellow, red, green, green, yellow, red, green, green, yellow, red, the core of the pattern is green, green, yellow, red.

Element in a Pattern: Elements of a pattern are the individual pieces. So green is an element of the pattern above. So is yellow and so is red.

Expression: An expression is a variable or combination of variables, numbers, and symbols that represents a mathematical relationship. For example, if we are calculating the cost of the school lunch for the entire class, we could say N = the number of students in the class and W = the cost of the lunch, so N x W would give you the total cost of all the lunches.

Formula: This is an equation that states a rule or fact. A formula is more formal than a rule and includes an equal sign. An example of a formula is Output = Input + 10.

Function: This is a relation where elements of one set are associated with elements of another set. For example, if you have boxes of pencils and each box has 12 pencils in it, we know that the total number of pencils is a function of the number of boxes.

Growing Patterns: These are patterns that don't just repeat. Instead they "grow." For example 2, 6, 10, 14, 18 is a growing pattern. It keeps growing by 4.

Recurring or Repeating Patterns: The elements of the pattern repeat. For example, AABCAABCAABC AABCAABC is a repeating pattern.

Rule in a Pattern: Growing patterns have rules that tell us how they grow. For example for the pattern 2, 6, 10, 14, 18, the rule is +4 because the pattern keeps growing by 4.

Variables: Sometimes we use a letter or symbol to stand for a quantity. For example, we could say $x \div 10 = 10$. We know that the value of x would be 100. Any letter can be used as a variable.

The Fantastic Five-Step Process

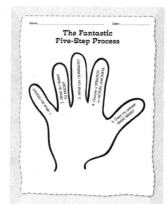

Problem solving is the first process standard listed in the National Council of Teachers Mathematics (NCTM) *Principles and Standards for Mathematics.* The accompanying statement reads, "Problem solving is an integral part of all mathematics learning. In everyday life and in the workplace, being able to solve problems can lead to great advantages. However, solving problems is not only a goal of learning mathematics but also a major means of doing so. Problem solving should not be an isolated part of the curriculum but should involve all Content Standards." In other words, in mathematics, problem solving is what it's all about!

What do you do when you first encounter a math word problem? This is what we need to help students deal with. We need to help them develop a process that they can use effectively to solve any type of math word problem. Word problems often intimidate students because there may be a lot of information, the information is embedded in text, and unlike a regular equation, it is not always clear exactly what you are supposed to do. When using these fill-in math word problems, you may want to take some time to teach (and subsequently review) the Fantastic Five-Step Process for problem solving.

The Fantastic Five-Step Process helps students approach problem solving in a logical, systematic way. No matter what type of problem students encounter, these five steps will help them through it. Learning and using the five steps will help students organize their interpretation and thinking about the problem. This is the key to good problem solving—organizing for action. The best way to help students understand the process is to demonstrate it as you work through a problem on the whiteboard or overhead. Make a copy of the graphic organizer on page 14. You can enlarge this to poster size or provide students with individual copies to follow along as you take them through an introductory lesson.

Step 1: What Do I Know?

Begin by writing a problem on the board or overhead—for example:

> Hit singer Fiona Arizona is unstoppable! She sold 1.5 million copies of her first album, which she recorded when she was just 15-years old. She was 16 when she came out with her next album, and that sold 3 million copies! She took the next year off to finish high school, then recorded her third album, which sold a record 6 million copies. Everyone is already predicting sales for her next album, due out next year. If the pattern continues, how many of this album will she sell?

Read the problem carefully. What are the facts? Have students volunteer these orally. Write them on the board:

Fiona made her first album when she was 15. First album sold 1.5 million copies. Released second album at age 16. The second album sold 3 million copies. Took a year off to finish school, then recorded third album. Third album sold 6 million copies.

Encourage students to write down the facts, too. This will help them focus on what's important while looking for ways to put it in a more accessible form. Can we arrange the facts in a way that will help us understand the problem situation? For example, maybe it would be good to draw what we know, or put it in a list, or make a table. Sometimes it's helpful to arrange numbers from lower to higher or higher to lower. In the case of Fiona Arizona, it might be helpful to organize the information in a chart.

First Album	Second Album	Third Album	Fourth Album
15 years old Sold 1.5 million copies.	16 years old Sold 3 million copies.	Took a year off to finish high school. Sold 6 million copies.	Due out in a year.

Step 2: What Do I Want to Know?

What is the question in the problem? What are we trying to find out? It's a good idea to have students state the question and also determine how the answer will be labeled. For example, if the answer is 100, 100 what? 100 hot dogs? 100 hit songs?

For this problem, we want to know one thing: How many copies of her fourth album can Fiona Arizona expect to sell? The answer will be labeled "albums."

Step 3: What Can I Eliminate?

Once we know what we are trying to find out, we can decide what is unimportant. You *may* need all the information, but often enough there is extra information that can be put aside to help focus on the facts. We can eliminate the facts related to Fiona's age, when each album came out, and what she did in between albums. That information is not needed to answer the question. We're left with the following:

First album: 1.5 million copies

Second album: 3 million copies

Third album: 6 million copies

Step 4: Choose a Strategy or Action and Solve.

Is there an action in the story (for example, is something being added) that will help the problem solver decide on an operation or a way to solve the problem?

$1.5 \times 2 = 3$ million albums

$3 \times 2 = 6$ million albums

Expressing this relationship with a variable, we might write $N \times 2 =$ sales of a new album, where $N =$ sales of previous album. To solve for sales of the fourth album, then, this is the action we need to do:

$6 \times 2 = 12$ million albums

So, to answer our question, "How many copies of her fourth album can Fiona Arizona expect to sell?" the answer is "12 million albums," because the pattern is that sales are doubling—sales of the second album are double the first, sales of the third album are double the second, and if we continue this pattern, sales of the fourth album will be double the third, 12 million albums.

Step 5: Does My Answer Make Sense?

Reread the problem. Look at the answer. Is it reasonable? Is it a sensible answer given what we know?

It makes sense for a number of reasons. First, we can see that Fiona's sales increase with each new album, so we know the answer has to be more than 6 million (sales of her most recent album). Since her new album sold 12 million copies, the answer is "yes"—the answer does make sense because 12 million is more than 6 million. The answer is also reasonable because the relationship between the numbers remains consistent. There is a growing pattern, with the sales doubling each time: 3 is double 1.5, 6 is double 3, and 12 is double 6, so the pattern holds.

Try a couple of sample word problems using this "talk-through" format with students. You might invite students to try the problem themselves first and then review it step-by-step together, sharing solutions to see if all steps were considered and if solutions are, in fact, correct. Practicing the process in this way helps make it part of a student's way of thinking mathematically.

Teaching Tip

Note that there are no answer keys for the fill-in math word problems as answers will vary depending on the numbers students supply to fill in the blanks. You might set up a buddy system for checking answers or have students turn in their stories for you to check. The fill-in stories provide good opportunities to reinforce strategies for determining if an answer is reasonable.

Meeting the Math Standards

The activities in this book include math content designed to support you in meeting the following math standards for algebra across grades 4–6, as outlined by the National Council of Teachers of Mathematics (NCTM) in *Principles and Standards for School Mathematics*.

Algebra

Understand patterns, relations, and functions

- sort, classify, and order objects by size, number, and other properties
- recognize, describe, and extend patterns
- analyze repeating and growing patterns

Represent and analyze mathematical situations and structures using algebraic symbols

- illustrate principles and properties of operations (such as commutativity)
- use invented and conventional symbolic notations
- use the properties of commutativity, associativity, and distributivity to compute with whole numbers
- use variables
- express mathematical relationships using equations

Use mathematical models to represent and understand quantitative relationships

- use objects, pictures, and symbols to model situations involving addition and subtraction of whole numbers
- model problems with objects; use graphs, tables, and equations to draw conclusions

The word problems in this book also support the NCTM process standards as follows:

Problem Solving

- solve problems that arise in mathematics and other contexts
- apply and adapt a variety of appropriate strategies to solve problems

Reasoning and Proof

- select and use various types of reasoning and methods of proof

Communication

- communicate mathematical thinking coherently and clearly

Connections

- understand how mathematical ideas interconnect and build on one another
- recognize and apply mathematics in contexts outside of mathematics

Representation

- create and use representations to organize, record, and communicate mathematical ideas
- use representations to model and interpret physical, social, and mathematical phenomena

Source: *Principles and Standards for School Mathematics* (National Council of Teachers of Mathematics, 2000-2004); www.standards.nctm.org.

Vocabulary-Building Connections

Take advantage of vocabulary-building opportunities that these fill-in stories present. For example, in "Too Much Homework!" (page 29), students will encounter the word *transfer*. Use words such as this to analyze word parts and origins. Using the word *transfer* as an example, have students look for word parts they recognize, such as the prefix *trans-*. Invite them to brainstorm other words that contain this word part, such as *transport* and *transform*. Investigate the origin and meaning of the word parts (Latin *trans*: across, beyond; and *-fer*, from Latin *ferre*, to carry). Have students use what they learn to determine the meaning of the word (*transfer*: to move someone or something from one place to another). Learning to break longer words into smaller, recognizable parts in this way and building knowledge of Greek and Latin roots boosts vocabulary development. Encourage students to analyze word parts on their own when they encounter unfamiliar words and to share what they learn.

Word Choice Chart

Type of Word	What It Is	More Examples
Adjective	A word that describes a noun or pronoun, such as *excited, impressive, purple,* and *peculiar.*	
Adverb	A word that tells where, how, or when, such as *outside, carefully,* and *soon.*	
Exclamation	A word that expresses something, like surprise, anger, or pain. Examples are *Oh, no!, Yeah!, Wow!,* and *Ugh!*	
Noun	A word that names a person, place, thing, or idea, such as *friend, city, skateboard,* and *friendship.*	
Plural Noun	A word that names more than one, such as *friends, cities, skateboards,* and *friendships.*	
Present-Tense Verb	A word that names an action, like *freeze, fly, sing,* and *sink.*	
Verb Ending in *-ing*	A word that tells what is happening, like *freezing, flying, singing,* and *sinking.*	
Past-Tense Verb	A word that tells what has already happened, like *froze, flew, sang* (or *sung*), *sank* (or *sunk*).	

The Fantastic
Five-Step Process

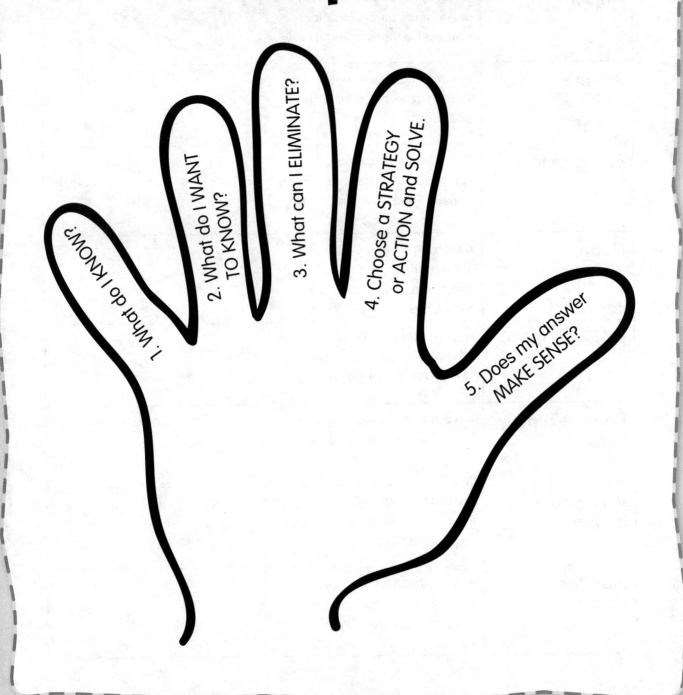

1. What do I KNOW?

2. What do I WANT TO KNOW?

3. What can I ELIMINATE?

4. Choose a STRATEGY or ACTION and SOLVE.

5. Does my answer MAKE SENSE?

Name: _____   Date: _____

Old Fairy Tale

Once upon a time, there was a little girl named

_____. She had one brother,
(first name of a girl)

_____. They lived in the _____
(first name of a boy)   (adjective)

forest with their _____ stepmother in a house made of
(adjective)

_____. She made them _____ and
(type of substance)   (present-tense verb)

_____ all day. One night, the stepmother sent the children
(present-tense verb)

out into the forest hoping they would get lost, but the boy secretly dropped a

small _____ behind him. Then the girl dropped a bit of
(noun)

_____. They took turns doing this, so that later they were
(noun)

able to follow the trail they made to get home. When they returned to the house,

they decided to run away to _____, where they lived
(name of a place)

_____ ever after.
(adjective ending in -ly)

Solve This!

What is the pattern of the trail?
Use letters to describe it. _____

Name: _____   Date: _____

Songwriter

I've decided I am going to be a songwriter

like _____. I just love
    (first and last name of a boy or girl)

songs like "The Wind Against My _____."
                       (body part)

That song makes me all _____. I am writing a song
                           (adjective)

now about _____. After the first verse, listeners will
           (plural noun)

hear a catchy chorus that goes like this: "_____,
                        (present-tense verb)

_____, _____." You repeat
  (present-tense verb)   (present-tense verb)

those words _____ times and follow it with a big bang on
      (number greater than 1)

the _____ to signal the start of the next verse. I
    (type of instrument)

think my song is going to be a big hit and I will be on the show *American*

_____!
   (noun)

Does this song follow an ABC pattern? _____

Explain. _____

Name: _____   Date: _____

Exercise Routine

To get in shape for the

_____ Olympics,
(name of a place)

_____ has developed
(first name of a girl)

a special exercise routine. She follows the same

routine every day. First she does _____
(number greater than 1)

_____-ups. Next she does _____
(present-tense verb)   (number greater than 1)

_____ jacks. Then she runs around her
(verb ending in -ing)

_____ _____ times. She repeats this
(noun)   (number greater than 1)

routine _____ times each day. She says it makes her feel
(number greater than 1)

_____. No doubt she will finish in _____
(adjective)   (ordinal number)

place in the Olympics this year.

Solve This!   What is the core
of this pattern? _____

Name: _____   Date: _____

Mysterious Border

We recently went to the village of _____ -istan
(last name of a student)

to explore ancient, _____ ruins with our
(adjective)

_____ professor, Dr. _____.
(adjective)   (first and last name of a student)

We found an old building that looked like it might have been the village's

_____. Carved into the border around the ceiling,
(type of building)

we noticed a fairly large _____, an upside-down
(noun)

_____, the letter _____, the
(noun)   (letter of the alphabet)

number _____, and a tiny _____. These
(any number)   (noun)

items were repeated _____ times to form the border. What
(number greater than 1)

could it mean? Our professor believes the ancient people were trying to contact

_____. Could be.
(plural noun)

What are the elements
of the pattern along the
ceiling border? _____

Name: _____ Date: _____

Working Hard at the Hotel

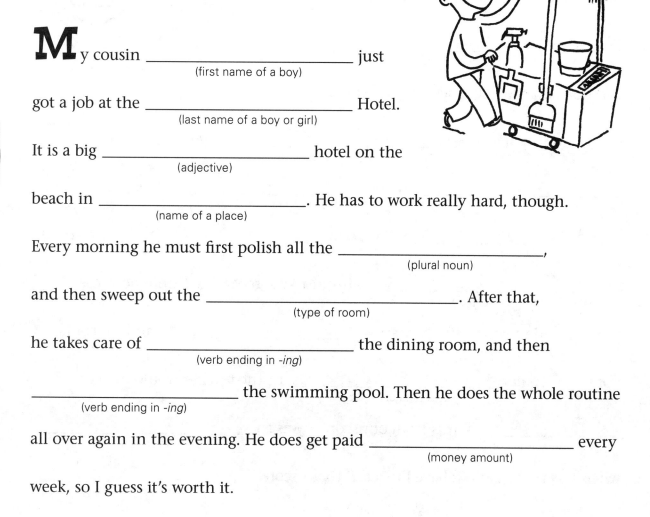

My cousin _____ just
(first name of a boy)

got a job at the _____ Hotel.
(last name of a boy or girl)

It is a big _____ hotel on the
(adjective)

beach in _____. He has to work really hard, though.
(name of a place)

Every morning he must first polish all the _____,
(plural noun)

and then sweep out the _____. After that,
(type of room)

he takes care of _____ the dining room, and then
(verb ending in -ing)

_____ the swimming pool. Then he does the whole routine
(verb ending in -ing)

all over again in the evening. He does get paid _____ every
(money amount)

week, so I guess it's worth it.

What is the pattern of the jobs? _____

Name: _____   Date: _____

The Big Test

We had a big test in class last week.

There were _____
(number greater than 50)

questions on the test. They were arranged

in a weird way. There were _____ questions about
(choose a number: 2, 3, or 4)

_____, then _____ questions about
(subject)   (choose a number: 2, 3, or 4)

_____, followed by _____ questions
(subject)   (choose a number: 2, 3, or 4)

about _____. This just kept repeating throughout the
(subject)

test. We had to write using a sharp _____, and we could
(noun)

not use a regular _____, or the teacher would deduct
(noun)

_____ points from our score. I was so _____
(number greater than 1)   (adjective)

when it was over, and relieved to learn that I scored _____
(number from 1 to 100)

percent on the test!

Solve This! Describe the pattern
of the questions using
the letters A, B, and C. _____

Name: _____   Date: _____

Fashion Designer

My cousin _____ is a fashion
(first name of a girl)

designer in _____. She designs
(name of a town)

clothes for people like _____ and
(name of a famous person)

_____. Of course, she has to wear fashionable
(name of a famous person)

clothes herself. She is very into three colors. She always wears

_____ one day, _____ the next
(color)   (color)

day, and _____ the day after that. She then repeats
(color)

this color sequence. She has shoes made of _____
(type of substance)

in different colors to match her clothes and she even wears coordinating

_____ hats. To pull everything together, she wears
(adjective)

coats made from _____ and designer jewelry by
(plural noun)

_____.
(name of a famous person)

Solve This!   What is the core of
the color pattern? _____

Name: _____ Date: _____

Coin Exhibit

_____ loves collecting
(first name of a boy)

coins. He recently put his collection of three

types of coins on display for all his friends.

He arranged them in rows with _____
(single-digit number greater than 1)

_____, then _____
(type of coin, plural)   (single-digit number greater than 1)

_____, followed by _____
(different type of coin, plural)   (single-digit number greater than 1)

_____ nickels. He repeated this arrangement with
(type of animal)

all of the coins. Then he stood back to admire his collection and said, "It

looks so _____ this way." I can't wait to see when he
(adjective)

displays his _____ collection! That should be even
(noun)

more _____.
(adjective)

Solve This!

What are the elements
of this pattern? _____

   50 Fill-In Math Word Problems: Algebra: Grades 4–6 © 2009 by Bob Krech and Joan Novelli, Scholastic Teaching Resources

Name: _____   Date: _____

Hit Song

That great rock group,

_____'s
(first name of a boy or girl)

_____, has released a new
(plural noun)

song. It is already a smash hit. The song is called "_____
(verb ending in -ing)

_____." It is so _____. The
(plural noun)   (adjective)

drummer bangs out a rhythm on the _____ that starts
(plural noun)

with 3 beats, then has 4, then 6, then 9, then 13. The beat goes on following this

pattern, with more and more beats. The rest of the band members are playing

_____ as loudly as they can. Of course they all wear
(musical instrument, plural)

_____ and _____. I can't wait to
(type of clothing)   (type of clothing)

see them in concert at the _____.
(name of a place)

Solve This!   What number would come
next in the beat pattern? _____

Name: _____ Date: _____

Lemonade Stand

_____'s
(first name of a girl that starts with the letter *L*)

_____ Lemonade Stand
(adjective that starts with the letter *L*)

opened over the weekend. It was a big success.

On Saturday, she sold _____ cups.
(double-digit number greater than 10)

On Sunday, that number doubled. On Monday, it doubled again. It might be so

popular because she uses _____ lemons and _____
(number greater than 1)   (number greater than 1)

teaspoons of sugar per cup. But I think the real reason is that she adds

_____ and _____ to every
(type of liquid)   (plural noun)

cup she pours. Without fail, her customers are _____
(verb ending in -*ed*)

when they find that at the bottom of their cup. It sure does make it taste

_____.
(adjective)

If the pattern continues, how
many cups of lemonade will be
sold on Wednesday? _____

  50 Fill-In Math Word Problems: Algebra: Grades 4–6 © 2009 by Bob Krech and Joan Novelli, Scholastic Teaching Resources

Name: _____   Date: _____

Concert Tour

The best band in the world,

the _____
                    (adjective)

_____, are on a concert
              (plural noun)

tour. Last _____
                  (day of the week)

they played in _____. They also sold
                      (name of a place)

_____ hot dogs at the concert to their hungry fans.
   (triple-digit number ending with 4)

The next day they played in _____, but
                                  (name of a place)

sold only half that number of hot dogs. The day after that they were in

_____, where they sold half the previous day's
         (name of a place)

number of hot dogs. Apparently, word is getting around that the band is great,

but the hot dogs are _____.
                              (adjective)

Solve This!   If the pattern continues,
how many hot dogs will the
band sell at the next concert? _____

Name: _____   Date: _____

My New Pet

I've got a new pet. He is a little unusual

because he is from _____.
                        (name of a planet)

I named him _____. He is
                (name of a famous person)

_____ feet tall and covered with _____ hair.
(number greater than 1)   (color)

My new pet eats a lot. The first day I had him, I gave him _____
                                                               (number greater than 1)

cans of dog food. He liked it. The next day he ate one more can than the day

before. He did the same thing every day for a week. Now he is so big I'll have to

build him his own _____ to live in. Of course, he is so
                       (type of building)

_____ I just have to keep him, even though he keeps me
        (adjective)

awake with his _____ at night.
                   (verb ending in -ing)

What is the rule for the eating pattern? _____

 50 Fill-In Math Word Problems: Algebra: Grades 4–6 © 2009 by Bob Krech and Joan Novelli, Scholastic Teaching Resources

Name: _____   Date: _____

Leaves, Leaves, Leaves!

A plant we are growing in science class is very

_____. Its botanical name is
     (adjective)

_____ *giganteus*. We give it
(last name of a famous person)

plenty of _____ and lots of _____
     (type of liquid)   (plural noun)

so that it will grow well. The plant grew _____ leaves on
                                       (single-digit number greater than 1)

each branch the first week. There were _____ branches. The
                                     (single-digit number greater than 1)

next week, the number of leaves tripled. And the week after that, the number of

leaves tripled again. Experts say the leaves from the plant can improve a person's

_____ ability. We even read a legend that says if you wear
     (verb ending in *-ing*)

the leaves around your _____ you will find your true
                         (body part)

_____.
     (noun)

Solve This! If the pattern continues, how many leaves will be on the plant in four weeks time? _____

50 Fill-In Math Word Problems: Algebra: Grades 4–6 © 2009 by Bob Krech and Joan Novelli, Scholastic Teaching Resources

Name: _____   Date: _____

Snowy Town

The town of _____ville
(last name of a boy or girl)

had record snowfalls again this year. That's not surprising, because the daily

temperature is usually no higher than about _____
(double-digit number)

degrees. People there have to wear _____ almost all
(type of clothing, plural)

year, and they have to dig out with their _____ almost
(type of tool, plural)

every morning. Their _____ get covered and they have
(plural noun)

to dig them out, too. It all started in _____. That year
(year before 2000)

they got _____ inches of snow. The snow was kind of
(single-digit number greater than 1)

_____, but it was still snow. The next year it snowed 4
(color)

times that. The following year it was 16 times as much, and the year after that it

was 30 times that amount! Even Mayor _____ said, "This is
(last name of a boy or girl)

_____!" He moved the next day.
(adjective)

Solve This! What is the rule for the
snowfall pattern? _____

50 Fill-In Math Word Problems: Algebra: Grades 4–6 © 2009 by Bob Krech and Joan Novelli, Scholastic Teaching Resources

Name: _____ Date: _____

Too Much Homework!

Our new teacher, Mr. _____,
(last name of a famous female)

is very tough. Every day we have to write _____ pages in our
(number greater than 1)

journals. We have to read _____ pages in our history books.
(number greater than 1)

We even have to clean our desks every morning, scrubbing them with

_____. But the worst is homework. The first day, our
(plural noun)

teacher gave us _____ pages of homework. Then when
(number greater than 10)

_____ complained, he said, "Tomorrow we will do ten
(first name of a boy or girl)

times that." When _____ said something about that, he
(first name of a boy or girl)

said, "Okay. On day three you'll have ten times that number of pages." Yikes!

I think I'll transfer to _____ School!
(last name of a famous person)

If the pattern continues, how many pages of
homework will they have on the fourth day?

_____

Growing Patterns

Skyscraper

The famous architect _____
(first and last name of a boy)

from _____ is designing a
(name of a country)

brand-new headquarters for the _____ Manufacturing
(last name of a boy or girl)

Company. As you know, this company manufactures _____.
(plural noun)

The building will be constructed with the finest materials, including

_____ and _____. The first floor will
(plural noun)   (plural noun)

be _____ meters high. The second floor increases in height
(number greater than 10)

by the square of the height of the first floor. In fact, all _____
(number greater than 1)

floors increase in height by the square of the previous floor! It is going to be a

_____ building! The ground floor will have shops like
(adjective)

_____ and _____. I can't wait
(name of a store)   (name of a store)

for it to be finished!

Solve This!   What will be the height
of the third floor? _____

Name: _____   Date: _____

Undersea Creature

An unusual undersea creature was recently

discovered on Planet _____ .
                        (last name of a boy or girl)

It is about _____ feet long and has
            (number greater than 1)

_____ and _____ stripes.
          (color)   (color)

Its head is shaped like a large _____ and it has
                                        (noun)

_____ eyes. When it wakes up in the morning, it immediately
(number greater than 1)

swims up _____ feet from the bottom, then down
              (number from 10 to 20)

_____ . It repeats this pattern until it reaches the surface,
(single-digit number greater than 5)

where it then rests for _____ minutes.
                          (number greater than 1)

Create a diagram or
graph to show the sea
creature's movement
after waking up.

50 Fill-In Math Word Problems: Algebra: Grades 4–6 © 2009 by Bob Krech and Joan Novelli, Scholastic Teaching Resources

Name: _____ Date: _____

Super Salesman

_____ is a super salesman.
(first and last name of a boy)

He sells _____ for the company
(plural noun)

_____, Incorporated. It is _____
(last name of a boy or girl)   (adjective)

work, and he has to travel and _____ a lot, but he loves it.
(present-tense verb)

He has _____ manners, which his customers appreciate.
(adjective)

In his first month he sold _____ units. His second-month sales
(number greater than 10)

increased by _____ times that amount. The third-month
(single-digit number greater than 1)

sales increased by twice the previous rate. The same thing happened again in

the fourth month. Because of this he was awarded an all-expenses-paid trip to

_____ and a gold _____. He is
(name of a place)   (noun)

certainly the most _____ salesman!
(adjective)

On the back of this paper, draw or graph the
number of units the salesman sold each month.

How many units did he sell
in the fourth month? _____

Name: _____   Date: _____

Bargain Hunter

My cousin _____ is a real
                    (first name of a girl)

bargain hunter. She goes to the regular stores like

_____ and _____, but she also goes
        (name of a store)   (name of a store)

to flea markets. She particularly likes to buy old _____.
                                                              (plural noun)

She saw one at the _____ Town Flea Market last week. She
                            (adjective)

loved it because it was _____ and old. In fact, it was from
                                (adjective)

_____. She offered the vendor _____. The
    (year before 2000)   (money amount less than $25)

vendor shook his head, "My price is firm. It's _____."
                                                  (money amount greater than $50)

My cousin figured she would need x more dollars to get it. She finally sold

two of her prized _____ figurines to get the
                            (plural noun)

extra money. She is happy, though, and has displayed her new piece on her

_____ at home.
        (type of furniture)

Solve This!   **What is the value of x?** _____

Using Variables

Space Travel

Starship Navigator _____
(last name of a boy or girl)

looked down at his instruments. "We have

approximately *n* solar miles to travel before we reach the moon of Planet

_____." They had already passed the Ring of
(last name of a boy or girl)

_____ and the Constellation _____
(last name of a boy or girl)   (last name of a boy or girl)

Major, the one shaped like a small _____. The commander
(noun)

of Starship _____, Captain_____,
(noun)   (last name of a boy or girl)

replied, "We've already traveled _____ solar miles, and that
(number from 1,000 to 4,998)

moon is _____ solar miles from Earth. I sure hope we see
(number from 5,000 to 10,000)

that _____ soon."
(noun)

Solve This!   What is the value of *n*? _____

 50 Fill-In Math Word Problems: Algebra: Grades 4–6 © 2009 by Bob Krech and Joan Novelli, Scholastic Teaching Resources

Name: _____ Date: _____

Sales Job

I just took a job selling very stylish

_____ to homeowners in
(plural noun)

our town of _____. Instead of selling them at a shop,
(name of a town)

I go door to door. Sometimes people don't want you to bother them. It can get a

little _____. They slam the _____
(adjective)   (noun)

in your face or tell you to "Go _____." But the pay is 20
(present-tense verb)

dollars an hour, which I think is pretty _____. I earned
(adjective)

_____ dollars the first week. So I don't care if
(choose a number: 100, 200, 300, 400, or 500)

someone isn't _____ and _____
(adjective)   (adjective)

when I try to sell them my product, because I'm going to earn enough to

buy the _____ I've always wanted. Then I'll be able to
(noun)

_____ every day.
(present-tense verb)

Solve This! If *n* = the number of hours worked,
what is the value of *n* in this story? _____

Name: _____ Date: _____

The Cup

My hockey team, the _____
(name of a town)

_____, just won the
(plural noun)

_____ Cup in the _____
(last name of a famous person)   (name of a place)

Hockey League. We beat our opponents, the _____
(name of a town)

_____, _____ to 0,
(type of animal, plural)   (single-digit number greater than 1)

even though their team won the award for the league's Most Valuable

_____. Along with the trophy cup, we also received
(noun)

_____ dollars. We shared the money evenly, which
(choose a number: 3,000, 4,000, or 5,000)

meant everyone on the team got _____ dollars. We played
(choose a number: 250 or 500)

well, maybe because we had our mascot, _____,
(name of a famous person)

cheering us on while wearing a furry _____ costume.
(type of animal)

If *x* = the number of people on the team,
what is the value of *x* in this story? _____

Name: _____   Date: _____

Monster Movie

_____ is a successful
(first and last name of a girl)

movie director. She did that movie

_____   _____ in Love.
(adjective)   (plural noun)

Her new movie is called _____ Monsters in
                         (adjective)

_____. She needed lots of cars for a scene where Godzilla
(name of a place)

runs across _____ parking lots, stepping on and crushing cars.
            (choose a number: 10, 20, or 50)

She had to get _____ cars for the scene and divide
               (choose a number: 1,000, 2,000, or 5,000)

them evenly among the parking lots. It was great! But not nearly as good as when

Godzilla fights King Kong on top of the _____.
                                          (name of a famous building)

They end up falling off and landing on the roof of _____.
                                                     (name of a restaurant)

Then they chase each other down _____ and end
                                 (name of a street)

up in _____. Now, that's _____!
       (body of water)   (adjective)

Solve This!

If *n* = the number of cars in a parking lot,

what is the value of *n* in this story? _____

Name: _____ Date: _____

She Loves Cats

My Aunt _____ loves
(first name of a girl)

cats, and she is very wealthy. She has more than

_____ dollars. She likes _____
(number greater than 1 million) (color)

cats and _____ cats. She likes _____
(color) (adjective)

ones and _____ ones, too. She had a special mansion
(adjective)

with _____ rooms built for her cats! There are
(choose a number: 40, 80, or 160)

_____ cats in each room. The rooms are all furnished
(choose a number: 2, 4, or 8)

with cat beds and lots of cat toys, like _____ and
(plural noun)

_____. The cats even have kitty _____
(plural noun) (type of clothing, plural)

hanging in their closets. My aunt's cats enjoy _____ every
(type of food)

day and they get plenty of _____ in their bowls. It's a pretty
(type of liquid)

_____ life being a cat with my aunt.
(adjective)

Solve This! If *c* = the number of cats in each room, what is the value of *c* in this story? _____

50 Fill-In Math Word Problems: Algebra: Grades 4–6 © 2009 by Bob Krech and Joan Novelli, Scholastic Teaching Resources

Name: _____   Date: _____

The Longest Beard

The _____ Book of World
     (last name of a famous person)

Records recently announced some new records. First,

_____ now holds the record for the longest hair. It is
(first and last name of a girl)

_____ inches long and a beautiful _____
(number greater than 1)   (color)

color. _____ was announced as having made the longest
      (first and last name of a boy)

paper chain. It is _____ inches long and it only took him
           (number greater than 1)

_____ hours to make it. Finally, _____ had
(number greater than 1)   (first and last name of a boy)

the longest beard. It was a record _____ inches long! It took
                   (choose a number: 50, 60, or 80)

him _____ days to grow it, and he said it grew at an even
   (choose a number: 2, 5, or 10)

rate. It was a really _____ _____
            (adjective)   (color)

color and very _____. People are starting to call him
          (adjective)

Old _____ Beard.
     (adjective)

Solve This!

If n = the number of inches of beard growth per day,
what is the value of n in this story? _____

50 Fill-In Math Word Problems: Algebra: Grades 4–6 © 2009 by Bob Krech and Joan Novelli, Scholastic Teaching Resources

Name: _____   Date: _____

Chocolate Lovers

We took at class trip to Chocolate World.

I think chocolate is _____! Chocolate World has all
(adjective)

kinds of chocolate. We saw chocolate _____ and
(plural noun)

chocolate _____. They even make chocolate with
(plural noun)

_____ in it and chocolate with _____
(type of food)   (plural noun)

on top. We watched the people working there make the chocolate. They stirred it

in big _____ with long _____.
(type of container, plural)   (plural noun)

Because our class was the lucky _____ class to visit, we were
(ordinal number)

given _____ ounces of chocolate! The
(choose a number: 100, 200, or 300)

_____ of us shared it equally. We ate most of it on the
(choose a number: 10, 20, 25, or 50)

_____ ride home to _____. It was
(type of vehicle)   (name of a town)

soooo _____!
(adjective)

 If *o* = the ounces of chocolate each student
received, what is the value of *o* in this story?

_____

Name: _____ Date: _____

Mail Carrier

_____ is a mail carrier in my
(first name of a boy)

neighborhood. Everyone likes him because he is so

_____. He always delivers the mail
(adjective)

by _____. _____ do not chase him the way
(time of day)   (type of animal, plural)

they do some mail carriers. He made friends with all of them by giving them

_____. He delivers mail to _____
(type of food)   (double-digit number)

houses in our neighborhood, which is called _____
(adjective)

Estates. Each day, he delivers _____ letters in only
(triple-digit number)

_____ hours. That's _____,
(single-digit number greater than 1)   (adjective)

of course, but we also like the way he is always _____
(verb ending in -ing)

and _____. He is the most _____
(verb ending in -ing)   (adjective)

mail carrier we've ever had.

Solve This!

Write an expression that describes how to find
how many letters the mail carrier delivers per hour.

_____

Name: _____   Date: _____

Fishing Trip

My Uncle _____
(first name of a boy)

took me and _____
(single-digit number greater than 1)

friends of mine on a fishing trip. We went

out on _____ in his boat, which was named the
(body of water)

_____   _____. We left at
(color)   (type of fish)

_____ and brought_____ sandwiches and
(time of day)   (type of food)

_____ to eat on the way out. Once we started fishing,
(type of food)

it was _____. We each caught _____
(adjective)   (double-digit number less than 20)

fish in only _____ hours! I guess we did so well because we
(number greater than 1)

used _____ for bait.
(plural noun)

Write an expression that describes how to find the
total number of fish they caught.

_____

   50 Fill-In Math Word Problems: Algebra: Grades 4–6 © 2009 by Bob Krech and Joan Novelli, Scholastic Teaching Resources

Name: _____ Date: _____

Comic Book Collection

My grandparents were cleaning out

their _____ attic. They found
(adjective)

some old _____ and some _____ that
(plural noun)   (plural noun)

Grandpa used in school. They also found my dad's old comic book collection. There

was a copy of _____-*Man #1* in mint condition! They also
(type of animal)

discovered the complete series of the *Fantastic* _____ *Girl* and
(noun)

_____ issues of _____-*Man*. My grandparents
(number greater than 1)   (noun)

decided to give all _____ comics to my _____
(triple-digit number)   (single-digit number greater than 1)

brothers and me. We promised to divide them up equally. I must say I really

want that issue of *Captain* _____, though. It is so
(noun)

_____. I hope I get it.
(adjective)

Solve This!

Write an expression that describes how to find the
number of comic books each sibling should get.

_____

Name: _____   Date: _____

The Donut Hike

I am a donut lover. I love _____
(flavor)

donuts and _____ donuts. I love
(type of food)

donuts with _____ icing and donuts
(color)

with _____ filling in the center.
(type of food)

I recently organized a new event, the Donut Hike. Over a course of

_____ miles, we hike from one donut shop to another.
(number greater than 1)

At each stop we eat one donut more than at the last place. We started at

_____'s Donut Den. I ate _____
(first name of a girl)   (single-digit number greater than 1)

donuts. We then went to _____ more places, ending up at
(single-digit number greater than 1)

_____'s Donut Palace. I think my favorite donut
(first name of a boy)

for the day was the Hot _____ _____
(flavor)   (type of fruit)

Donut. That was amazingly _____!
(adjective)

Write an expression that describes how to determine
how many donuts were eaten.

_____

Name: _____ Date: _____

Onion Cooking Contest

Chef _____ just held her
(first and last name of a girl)

First Annual Onion Cooking Contest. She had _____
(triple-digit number)

onions and there were three contestants: _____,
(first and last name of a boy or girl)

_____, and _____. Each
(first and last name of a boy or girl)   (name of a famous person)

contestant had to create a delicious and _____
(adjective)

onion dish using onions, of course, along with other ingredients like

_____ and _____. Each contestant
(plural noun)   (type of substance)

used _____ onions per hour. The contestants cooked
(single-digit number greater than 1)

for _____ hours. The chef sampled each dish and
(single-digit number greater than 1)

finally awarded the prize to the contestant who prepared Baked Onions With

_____ Sauce. The prize was an all-expenses-paid trip
(noun)

to _____.
(name of a place)

Solve This!

Write an expression that describes how to find the
number of onions left.

_____

Name: _____   Date: _____

Tale of the Gold

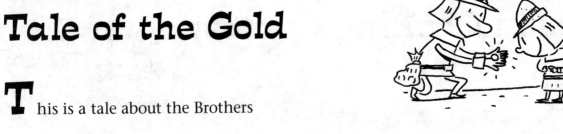

This is a tale about the Brothers

_____. They lived with their father,
(last name of a boy or girl)

_____, and mother, _____, in an
(first name of a boy)   (first name of a girl)

old _____ castle in _____. There
(adjective)   (name of a town)

were _____ brothers in all. When they were preparing to
(number from 5 to 9)

leave home to go out into the world, the father gave the first one a gold coin

and a single _____ _____.
(adjective)   (noun)

The second brother left and got one more gold coin than the first and a tiny

_____ _____. And so it went. Each
(adjective)   (noun)

brother got one more gold coin than the previous brother. They used their gold to

build _____ that everyone _____.
(plural noun)   (verb ending in -ed)

Write an expression that shows how to find the total
number of gold pieces the brothers received.

_____

Name: _____   Date: _____

Reading Calendar

My teacher, Mr. _____,
(last name of a boy or girl)

is a bit _____. He gave our
(adjective)

class a one-week reading calendar to complete. He said we should start on

the first night by reading the same number of pages as our age. Every night

after that, he said, we should double the number of pages we read. I started

with "The Three Little _____." Then I read "Little
(type of animal, plural)

_____ Riding _____." I finished up
(color)   (type of clothing)

with "The Adventures of _____."
(name of a famous person)

While I read, I had a snack of _____ cookies each night, along
(number greater than 1)

with a glass of _____. It was good, but it made me feel
(type of liquid)

pretty _____.
(adjective)

Solve This!   Write an expression that shows how to find the total
number of pages read in a week.

_____

Name: _____   Date: _____

Party Planner

_____ is helping her Aunt
(first and last name of a girl)

_____ plan a big party. She
(first name of a girl)

arranged for the band the _____
                                    (verb ending in -ing)

_____ to play the music. She also ordered a fancy
(plural noun)

_____ cake that is _____ feet long
(flavor)   (single-digit number greater than 1)

and shaped like an actual _____. Of course, she is having
                                    (noun)

_____ guests, so she needs a lot of cake. Each guest will also get a
(number greater than 1)

crystal _____ filled with _____ mints.
              (type of container)   (number greater than 1)

In fact, guests who are older than _____ will get
                                          (double-digit number)

double the number of mints. It really is going to be a super

_____ party!
(adjective)

Solve This!

Write expressions that describe how to find the
number of mints each guest will get.

_____

_____

   50 Fill-In Math Word Problems: Algebra: Grades 4–6 © 2009 by Bob Krech and Joan Novelli, Scholastic Teaching Resources

Name: _____   Date: _____

Weight-Lifting Competition

The _____
(last name of a boy or girl)

County Weight-Lifting Championships were held this weekend in

_____ Arena. Each weightlifter had to lift
(last name of a boy or girl)

_____ times his or her body weight. That is not as
(single-digit number greater than 1)

_____ as you might think. The top two lifters turned out to
(adjective)

be _____ and _____. First prize was
(first and last name of a boy or girl)   (first and last name of a boy or girl)

a brand-new electric_____. Second prize was dinner for two
(noun)

at _____'s Restaurant. Throughout the competition, there
(first and last name of a boy)

was a lot of _____ and _____, but in
(verb ending in -ing)   (verb ending in -ing)

the end, it was a very _____ event!
(adjective)

Solve This! Write a formula to describe how to determine
how much weight each weightlifter had to lift.

_____

Name: _____ Date: _____

Concert Tour

One of _____'s
          (name of a country)

best bands, _____
                    (color)

_____, recently toured _____.
          (noun)   (name of a state in the U.S.)

In all, the band played _____ concerts. Each night
                        (single-digit number greater than 1)

they played their most popular song, "_____ the
                                       (present-tense verb)

_____." They also played _____
          (noun)   (double-digit number less than 50)

other songs, some of which were _____ minutes long! Their lead
                                (number greater than 1)

singer, _____, also known as _____-O,
        (first and last name of a boy)   (noun)

wore his famous black _____ on his head. All the fans
                              (noun)

shouted, "_____," whenever he came on stage. It was the
                  (expression)

band's most _____ tour ever!
                    (adjective)

Write a formula to find the number of songs the
band played on the tour.

_____

Name: _____   Date: _____

Clubhouse

My friends _____ and
(first name of a boy or girl)

_____ and I are building a
(first name of a boy or girl)

clubhouse for our Be Kind to _____ Club.
(plural noun)

We painted the walls _____ and put up paintings
(color)

of _____. We put in _____ windows
(plural noun)   (number greater than 1)

and added a roof made of _____, so it all looks pretty
(type of substance)

_____. Now we have to put carpet on the floor. We chose
(adjective)

_____ carpet because it looks so _____.
(color)   (adjective)

The room is _____ feet long and _____ feet wide. The
(double-digit number)   (double-digit number)

whole area has to be carpeted because we want to _____
(present-tense verb)

and _____ in the clubhouse. I can't wait for our first
(present-tense verb)

meeting. Our guest speaker is _____!
(name of a famous person)

Solve This!   Write a formula to find how
much carpet they need. _____

Name: _____ Date: _____

Island Visit

Our family recently flew to the island of

_____ for a vacation. The
(last name of a boy or girl)

flight was _____ hours long, but it was worth it.
(number greater than 1)

There were _____ beaches, where we could
(adjective)

_____ as much as we wanted. There were even
(present-tense verb)

_____ fruit trees, which are pretty rare. I noticed
(noun)

each tree had _____ branches and each branch had
(single-digit number greater than 1)

_____ fruits on it. There were only _____
(single-digit number greater than 1)   (number greater than 1)

of these trees on the island. We also played some golf, but the courses had

_____ holes and we had to use our _____ to
(number greater than 1)   (noun)

hit the ball. It really was a very _____ kind of place.
(adjective)

Write a formula to determine how much fruit
was on the trees.

_____

Name: _____   Date: _____

Expressions and Formulas

Socks for the Team

Our soccer team, the _____
(name of a town)

_____, just ordered new uniforms.
(plural noun)

There are _____ of us and we are all
(double-digit number less than 25)

really _____ about this. We chose the
(adjective)

_____ uniforms with _____
(color)   (color)

sleeves. We decided to put a big _____ on the front of
(type of animal)

the shirts. Our uniforms will include shirts, shorts, and socks. The socks are

_____ with _____ stripes. We had to
(color)   (color)

order _____ pairs of socks for each player because we wear
(single-digit number greater than 1)

them out so fast. When the uniforms arrive, we will have to try them on to make

sure they look _____. I can't wait for our first game against
(adjective)

_____. We will _____ them!
(name of a town)   (present-tense verb)

Solve This! Write a formula to determine how many
socks the team should order. _____

Expressions and Formulas

Tickets for the Play

My mom and dad got tickets for us all to go

see a new play, *The* _____

(adjective)

Detective, at the _____

(last name of a boy or girl)

Theater in _____. It is a mystery, so I'm sure I will

(name of a place)

_____ it. All _____ of us in our

(present-tense verb)   (number from 3 to 8)

family are going. The tickets are _____ dollars each. There is

(number greater than 1)

also a handling fee of _____ dollars for each ticket. I'm

(single-digit number greater than 1)

sure the show will be worth it, though. _____

(first and last name of a girl)

and _____ are starring in it, and they are both

(name of a famous actor)

so _____.

(adjective)

Write a formula to find the total amount
paid for the tickets.

_____

Name: _____   Date: _____

Gold Mine!

What an incredible discovery!

There was a gold mine right under _____.
(name of a school)

Mr. _____ found it when one of the
(last name of a boy)

_____ we were playing with rolled out of sight during
(plural noun)

recess. When he went to get it, he discovered a large hole in the ground. He

led a group of _____ of us down into a tunnel he dug
(double-digit number less than 20)

with a gas-powered _____. About _____
(type of tool)   (number greater than 1)

feet into the tunnel, we unearthed _____ pounds of
(double-digit number greater than 20)

gold. Our teacher decided the students would all share it equally. I was so

_____ that I could barely _____. I
(adjective)   (present-tense verb)

can finally afford to buy the new _____ I've been wanting.
(noun)

Solve This!

Write a formula to determine how much gold each
student should get.

_____

---

50 Fill-In Math Word Problems: Algebra: Grades 4–6 © 2009 by Bob Krech and Joan Novelli, Scholastic Teaching Resources

Name: _____   Date: _____

Drive-In Movie

My family went to the drive-in movie

theater last night. We saw *Revenge of the*

_____. It was really
(plural noun)

_____. We got popcorn and _____
(adjective)   (type of food)

from the snack bar. There were a lot of people there. In fact, there were

_____ rows of cars with _____
(double-digit number less than 40)   (double-digit number less than 40)

cars in each row. I slept for about _____ minutes during the
                                              (number greater than 1)

movie, but woke up just at the part where the _____ comes
                                                                  (noun)

to get the actress, _____. Fortunately, she is saved
                          (first and last name of a girl)

by the hero, played by _____. Wow! That movie
                              (first and last name of a boy)

was totally_____!
                    (adjective)

Write a formula that shows how to find the total
number of cars at the drive-in.

_____

Equations and Properties

Pet Show

I entered my pet bunny,

_____, in the
(first name of a boy or girl)

_____ Pet Show. There were lots of different pets.
(name of a place)

_____ brought her pet _____.
(first name of a girl)   (type of animal)

_____ had his pet _____.
(first name of a boy)   (type of animal)

There were some cool dogs, too. One of them could actually

_____ _____. There were
(present-tense verb)   (plural noun)

_____ entries in the show and every other one was a bunny!
(even number from 50 to 100)

Of course, my pet bunny stood out because she can _____
                                                                        (present-tense verb)

_____. You have to admit, that really is a talent. In fact, she
(plural noun)

won the Golden _____ for Best Bunny in Show.
                                (noun)

Solve This!   Write an equation that determines how many bunnies were at the show.

_____

Name: _____ Date: _____

Earning a Bike

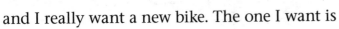

My name is _____
(first name of a boy)

and I really want a new bike. The one I want is

the _____ Speedster.
(last name of a boy or girl)

It is a really _____ bike so you can see why it
(adjective)

costs _____. I have a job _____
(money amount over $20) (verb ending in -ing)

_____ at the _____
(plural noun) (color)

_____ Restaurant. The pay is _____ an hour.
(type of animal) (money amount under $5)

My boss, Mr. _____, is kind of tough.
(last name of a boy)

He makes me wear _____ at work and is always telling
(type of clothing)

me to _____ when I am around the customers. But he does
(present-tense verb)

give me plenty of hours and I get all the _____ I want to eat!
(type of food)

Write an equation that determines how long the boy
has to work to get the bike.

_____

Name: _____   Date: _____

Fantastic Pudding

We went on a class trip to the

_____ Pudding Factory
(last name of a boy or girl)

last week. We got to see how they make pudding and how they

_____ it. There were lots of flavors, like _____,
(present-tense verb)   (type of food)

_____, and _____. I tasted some and
(type of food)   (type of food)

it was _____. There were _____
(adjective)   (double-digit number less than 30)

of us on the trip, including our teachers, Ms. _____ and
(last name of a girl)

Mr. _____. At the end of the pudding factory tour, the
(last name of a famous male)

president of the company gave our class a big container of pudding that weighed

_____ pounds. We all split it up evenly and ate it on the
(double-digit number greater than 50)

_____ all the way home.
(mode of transportation)

Solve This!

Write an equation that determines the amount
of pudding each person got.

_____

Name: _____ Date: _____

New Playground

Mr. _____ took
(last name of a boy)

his first-grade class outside to have fun on the

new playground. There were _____
(type of animal)

bars, slides, and an awesome _____ pit. There was
(type of substance)

also a seesaw made of _____. This playground is really
(type of building material)

_____! There are _____
(adjective)   (double-digit even number between 20 and 30)

first graders, and they all piled onto the seesaw. One side had

_____ kids on it. When the teacher saw them, he said,
(single-digit even number)

"Hey, you need to _____ that seesaw or you will
(present-tense verb)

_____!"
(present-tense verb)

Write an equation to show how the sides of the
seesaw could be balanced with the same number of
first graders on each side.

_____

Name: _____   Date: _____

Candy-Making Contest

The First Annual _____
(name of a town)

Candy-Making Contest took place this weekend

at the _____ Cooking School.
(last name of a boy or girl)

It was Chef _____ against Chef _____. The
(first and last name of a girl)   (first and last name of a boy)

candy they each had to make was Chocolate-Covered _____,
(plural noun)

everyone's favorite! The first chef up made _____ pieces
(double-digit number)

of candy per hour and worked for _____ hours. The
(single-digit number greater than 1)

second chef made _____ pieces per hour and worked for
(same single-digit number as before)

_____ hours. It was an incredibly _____
(same double-digit number as before)   (adjective)

contest and the candy, of course, tasted _____!
(adjective)

Solve This!

What property of multiplication could be applied here? Write an equation that fits this story and demonstrates this property.

_____

Name: _____ Date: _____

Hat Collector

My Uncle _____ is a hat collector.
(first name of a boy)

He also collects _____, but hats are
(plural noun)

his passion. He has a hat that is _____ years
(number greater than 1)

old and he also has a hat worn by _____. He has a hat
(name of a famous person)

that has _____ coming out of the top and one that
(plural noun)

is made of _____. Recently, he went looking for hats
(type of substance)

in our _____. He found lots of hatboxes. On the first
(type of room)

day, he opened _____ boxes and discovered one hat in each
(number greater than 10)

box. He looked for three more days and opened _____ boxes,
(number greater than 1)

but found zero hats. Still, he was very _____ and wore
(adjective)

_____ of the hats when he finally went home.
(single-digit number greater than 1)

What property of addition could be applied here? Write an equation that fits the story and demonstrates this property.

_____

Name: _____   Date: _____

Hall of Fame

We have a new member of our Sports Hall

of Fame here in _____.
                        (name of a town)

It is basketball player _____.
                              (first and last name of a boy)

He is even better than _____. It's not just because
                              (name of a famous person)

he can jump _____ feet high or that he can run a mile in
                  (number greater than 1)

_____ minutes. He scored _____ points in
  (number greater than 1)   (double-digit number)

one game against the _____ _____!
                            (name of another town)   (name of an animal)

He never did it again. In fact, he never scored again, but still that was

totally _____. Also, I think he switched over to
              (adjective)

_____.
  (type of sport)

What property of multiplication could be applied
here? Write an equation that fits this story and
demonstrates this property.

_____

Name: _____   Date: _____

Equations and Properties

Classroom Challenge

There are two teams in our Classroom

Challenge. One team is called the

_____ and the other is
(plural noun)

the _____.
(plural noun)

We have to answer questions about _____
(plural noun)

and _____, and we score points for correct answers.
(plural noun)

We're going to have the contest in the _____,
(room in a school)

and _____ will be in charge. So far, our team
(name of a famous person)

has _____ boys and _____
(single-digit number greater than 1)   (single-digit number greater than 1)

girls. The second team has 21 players. The grand prize is a trip to

_____, so you know we really want to win!
(name of a place)

Write an equation to show
how to make the teams even. _____

50 Fill-In Math Word Problems: Algebra: Grades 4–6 © 2009 by Bob Krech and Joan Novelli, Scholastic Teaching Resources